Dear users of this book,

We are pleased that our unique product has reached your hands. Thanks to our everyday Q&A process, you will deepen your relationship and strengthen the love between you. During this full-year experience you will be able to get to know each other better, no matter how long your relationship is!

We wish you a lot of joy during each of these 365 days. Let this time be a wonderful adventure for you!

Lovofun Team

HOW TO USE THIS BOOK?

Write down the date here

Question of the day

Date:
....

What is your biggest dream?

Person 1:

Person 2:

Place for your answers. Write as much as possible, even if the question is simple.
Explain why you choose this kind of answer.

Are you ready?

Date:

....

What makes you happy?

Person 1:

_____
_____
_____
_____
_____
_____
_____

Person 2:

_____
_____
_____
_____
_____
_____

Date:

....

Imagine that today is your last day. What are you going to do?

Person 1:

_____

_____

_____

_____

_____

_____

_____

Person 2:

_____

_____

_____

_____

_____

_____

Date:

....

What intrigued you most in your partner during the first meeting?

Person 1:

_____
_____
_____
_____
_____
_____
_____

Person 2:

_____
_____
_____
_____
_____

Date:

....

What is your favorite dish?

Person 1:

_____
_____
_____
_____
_____
_____
_____
_____

Person 2:

_____
_____
_____
_____
_____
_____

What do you like to do most in your free time?

Person 1:

_____

_____

_____

_____

_____

_____

_____

Person 2:

_____

_____

_____

_____

_____

_____

Date:

....

What annoys you the most?

Person 1:

_____

_____

_____

_____

_____

_____

_____

Person 2:

_____

_____

_____

_____

_____

What is your dream gift?

Person 1:

_____

_____

_____

_____

_____

_____

_____

Person 2:

_____

_____

_____

_____

_____

_____

Date:

....

Where would you like to go together?

Person 1:

_____
_____
_____
_____
_____
_____
_____

Person 2:

_____
_____
_____
_____
_____
_____

Date:

....

What is your biggest dream?

Person 1:

_____

_____

_____

_____

_____

_____

_____

Person 2:

_____

_____

_____

_____

_____

_____

Date:

....

Children - what do you think about when hearing this word?

Person 1:

_____

_____

_____

_____

_____

_____

_____

_____

Person 2:

_____

_____

_____

_____

_____

_____

Date:

....

How does your dream date look like?

Person 1:

_____
_____
_____
_____
_____
_____
_____

Person 2:

_____
_____
_____
_____
_____
_____

What do you like most about your partner?

Person 1:

_____
_____
_____
_____
_____
_____
_____

Person 2:

_____
_____
_____
_____
_____
_____

How do you imagine yourself in 10 years?

Person 1:

_____
_____
_____
_____
_____
_____
_____

Person 2:

_____
_____
_____
_____
_____
_____

Date:

....

You are going to a desert island - choose one thing to take for your partner.

Person 1:

_____
_____
_____
_____
_____
_____
_____

Person 2:

_____
_____
_____
_____
_____
_____

What is your partner's most commonly used word?

Person 1:

_____

_____

_____

_____

_____

_____

_____

Person 2:

_____

_____

_____

_____

_____

Date:

....

What does your partner do when he is happy?

Person 1:

_____
_____
_____
_____
_____
_____
_____

Person 2:

_____
_____
_____
_____
_____
_____
_____

Date:

....

What is your favorite drink?

Person 1:

_____
_____
_____
_____
_____
_____
_____

Person 2:

_____
_____
_____
_____
_____

Date:

....

What made you decide to have a relationship with your partner?

Person 1:

_____
_____
_____
_____
_____
_____
_____
_____

Person 2:

_____
_____
_____
_____
_____
_____
_____

What do you dislike most about your partner?

Person 1:

_____
_____
_____
_____
_____
_____
_____

Person 2:

_____
_____
_____
_____
_____
_____

Date:

....

What does your partner do when she/he is sad?

Person 1:

_____
_____
_____
_____
_____
_____
_____

Person 2:

_____
_____
_____
_____
_____
_____

Date:

....

How do you imagine your family in the future?

Person 1:

_____

_____

_____

_____

_____

_____

_____

Person 2:

_____

_____

_____

_____

_____

Date:

....

Who did you want to be when you were a child?

Person 1:

_____
_____
_____
_____
_____
_____
_____

Person 2:

_____
_____
_____
_____
_____

What love means to you?

Person 1:

_____

_____

_____

_____

_____

_____

_____

Person 2:

_____

_____

_____

_____

_____

_____

Date:

....

What color do you associate with your partner?

Person 1:

_____
_____
_____
_____
_____
_____
_____

Person 2:

_____
_____
_____
_____
_____
_____

Date:

....

What is your favorite animal?

Person 1:

_____

_____

_____

_____

_____

_____

_____

Person 2:

_____

_____

_____

_____

_____

If you had met your partner for the first time once again, what would you have told him?

Person 1:

_____
_____
_____
_____
_____
_____
_____

Person 2:

_____
_____
_____
_____
_____
_____

Date:

....

What does happiness mean to you?

Person 1:

_____

_____

_____

_____

_____

_____

_____

Person 2:

_____

_____

_____

_____

_____

Date:

....

What is your first association with your partner?

Person 1:

_____

_____

_____

_____

_____

_____

_____

Person 2:

_____

_____

_____

_____

_____

_____

Date:

....

What are your dream holidays?

Person 1:

_____
_____
_____
_____
_____
_____
_____

Person 2:

_____
_____
_____
_____
_____
_____

Date:

....

What is your favorite name?

Person 1:

_____

_____

_____

_____

_____

_____

_____

Person 2:

_____

_____

_____

_____

_____

Date:

....

Who is God
to you?

Person 1:

_____
_____
_____
_____
_____
_____
_____

Person 2:

_____
_____
_____
_____
_____

Date:

....

What do you value most in your partner?

Person 1:

_____

_____

_____

_____

_____

_____

_____

Person 2:

_____

_____

_____

_____

_____

_____

You win $ 1,000,000, what are you doing?

Person 1:

_____

_____

_____

_____

_____

_____

_____

Person 2:

_____

_____

_____

_____

_____

Are you satisfied with your life?

Person 1:

_____
_____
_____
_____
_____
_____
_____

Person 2:

_____
_____
_____
_____
_____
_____

Date:

....

What is your favorite thing in your home?

Person 1:

_____
_____
_____
_____
_____
_____
_____

Person 2:

_____
_____
_____
_____
_____

Date:

....

What animal do you associate with your partner?

Person 1:

_____

_____

_____

_____

_____

_____

Person 2:

_____

_____

_____

_____

_____

_____

Date:

....

What is your most valuable souvenir related to your relationship?

Person 1:

_____

_____

_____

_____

_____

_____

_____

Person 2:

_____

_____

_____

_____

_____

_____

Give 3 words that describe your partner.

Person 1:

_____

_____

_____

_____

_____

_____

Person 2:

_____

_____

_____

_____

_____

_____

Give 3 words that describe you.

Person 1:

_____

_____

_____

_____

_____

_____

_____

Person 2:

_____

_____

_____

_____

_____

Date:

....

What is your greatest memory of your relationship?

Person 1:

_____

_____

_____

_____

_____

_____

_____

Person 2:

_____

_____

_____

_____

_____

_____

Date:

....

What is your dream job?

Person 1:

_____

_____

_____

_____

_____

_____

_____

Person 2:

_____

_____

_____

_____

_____

_____

Date:

....

What would you like to change in your life?

Person 1:

_____
_____
_____
_____
_____
_____
_____

Person 2:

_____
_____
_____
_____
_____
_____

What do you value most in people?

Person 1:

_____

_____

_____

_____

_____

_____

_____

Person 2:

_____

_____

_____

_____

_____

_____

Date:

....

What plant do you associate with your partner?

Person 1:

_____
_____
_____
_____
_____
_____
_____

Person 2:

_____
_____
_____
_____
_____
_____

If you had to move abroad, which country would you choose?

Person 1:

_____

_____

_____

_____

_____

_____

_____

Person 2:

_____

_____

_____

_____

_____

What do you like about yourself the most?

Person 1:

_____

_____

_____

_____

_____

_____

_____

Person 2:

_____

_____

_____

_____

_____

Date:

....

What does money mean for you?

Person 1:

_____

_____

_____

_____

_____

_____

_____

Person 2:

_____

_____

_____

_____

_____

_____

What does happiness mean to you?

Person 1:

_____
_____
_____
_____
_____
_____
_____

Person 2:

_____
_____
_____
_____
_____
_____
_____

Date:

....

What are you grateful for to your partner?

Person 1:

_____

_____

_____

_____

_____

_____

_____

Person 2:

_____

_____

_____

_____

_____

_____

Date:

....

What is your unfulfilled childhood dream?

Person 1:

_____
_____
_____
_____
_____
_____
_____

Person 2:

_____
_____
_____
_____
_____
_____
_____

What are you grateful for to yourself?

Person 1:

_____

_____

_____

_____

_____

_____

_____

Person 2:

_____

_____

_____

_____

_____

_____

Date:

....

What will happen after death?

Person 1:

_____
_____
_____
_____
_____
_____
_____
_____

Person 2:

_____
_____
_____
_____
_____
_____

How did you imagine your future husband / wife in your childhood?

Person 1:

_____
_____
_____
_____
_____
_____
_____

Person 2:

_____
_____
_____
_____
_____
_____

Date:

....

What is faith for you?

Person 1:

_____
_____
_____
_____
_____
_____
_____

Person 2:

_____
_____
_____
_____
_____
_____

Is your partner's work interesting?

Person 1:

_____

_____

_____

_____

_____

_____

_____

Person 2:

_____

_____

_____

_____

_____

_____

Imagine you are switching roles with your partner. What would be your first action?

Person 1:

_____

_____

_____

_____

_____

_____

_____

Person 2:

_____

_____

_____

_____

_____

_____

Date:

....

How did you imagine your future family as a child?

Person 1:

_____

_____

_____

_____

_____

_____

_____

Person 2:

_____

_____

_____

_____

_____

How much would you like to earn?

Person 1:

_____
_____
_____
_____
_____
_____
_____

Person 2:

_____
_____
_____
_____
_____
_____
_____

Date:

....

List three reasons why you like your partner.

Person 1:

_____

_____

_____

_____

_____

_____

_____

Person 2:

_____

_____

_____

_____

_____

_____

Do you believe in male--female friendship?

Person 1:

_____
_____
_____
_____
_____
_____
_____

Person 2:

_____
_____
_____
_____
_____
_____

Date:

....

What is your favorite book?

Person 1:

_____

_____

_____

_____

_____

_____

_____

Person 2:

_____

_____

_____

_____

_____

What should your partner do to be a better person?

Person 1:

_____
_____
_____
_____
_____
_____
_____

Person 2:

_____
_____
_____
_____
_____
_____

If you have children - how do you imagine their future? If you don't have, how do you imagine them?

Person 1:

_____

_____

_____

_____

_____

_____

_____

Person 2:

_____

_____

_____

_____

_____

_____

Your partner is master in ...?

Person 1:

_____
_____
_____
_____
_____
_____
_____

Person 2:

_____
_____
_____
_____
_____
_____

What is your partner's most common curse?

Person 1:

_____

_____

_____

_____

_____

_____

_____

Person 2:

_____

_____

_____

_____

_____

_____

Imagine you are 90 years old. What do you feel in your heart, do you regret not doing something?

Person 1:

_____
_____
_____
_____
_____
_____
_____

Person 2:

_____
_____
_____
_____
_____
_____

What was the first word of your child? If you don't have children, what would you like it to be?

Person 1:

_____

_____

_____

_____

_____

_____

_____

Person 2:

_____

_____

_____

_____

_____

_____

Date:

....

What would you like to do in bed, but you're ashamed to say it?

Person 1:

_____

_____

_____

_____

_____

_____

_____

Person 2:

_____

_____

_____

_____

_____

_____

What language have you always wanted to learn?

Person 1:

_____

_____

_____

_____

_____

_____

_____

Person 2:

_____

_____

_____

_____

_____

Date:

....

What is your favorite movie?

Person 1:

_____
_____
_____
_____
_____
_____
_____

Person 2:

_____
_____
_____
_____
_____
_____

Date:

....

What do you like most about foreplay?

Person 1:

_____
_____
_____
_____
_____
_____
_____

Person 2:

_____
_____
_____
_____
_____

What song do you associate with your partner?

Person 1:

_____
_____
_____
_____
_____
_____
_____

Person 2:

_____
_____
_____
_____
_____
_____

Pizza with or without pineapple?

Person 1:

_____

_____

_____

_____

_____

_____

Person 2:

_____

_____

_____

_____

_____

_____

Date:

....

What is your favorite series?

Person 1:

_____

_____

_____

_____

_____

_____

_____

_____

Person 2:

_____

_____

_____

_____

_____

_____

Date:

....

Sex outside the home: where would you like to try?

Person 1:

_____
_____
_____
_____
_____
_____
_____

Person 2:

_____
_____
_____
_____
_____

Date:

....

What music do you like?

Person 1:

_____
_____
_____
_____
_____
_____
_____

Person 2:

_____
_____
_____
_____
_____
_____

What is your favorite fast food?

Person 1:

_____
_____
_____
_____
_____
_____
_____

Person 2:

_____
_____
_____
_____
_____

What is your favorite fairy tale character?

Person 1:

_____
_____
_____
_____
_____
_____
_____

Person 2:

_____
_____
_____
_____
_____
_____
_____

Date:

....

Would you prefer to be burned or buried in a coffin?

Person 1:

_____

_____

_____

_____

_____

_____

_____

Person 2:

_____

_____

_____

_____

_____

_____

Date:

....

Do you brush your teeth before or after breakfast?

Person 1:

_____
_____
_____
_____
_____
_____
_____

Person 2:

_____
_____
_____
_____
_____
_____
_____

What is the unhealthy thing to eat that you like most?

Person 1:

_____

_____

_____

_____

_____

_____

_____

Person 2:

_____

_____

_____

_____

_____

What is your favorite sex position?

Person 1:

_____

_____

_____

_____

_____

_____

Person 2:

_____

_____

_____

_____

_____

What is your favorite superhero?

Person 1:

_____
_____
_____
_____
_____
_____
_____

Person 2:

_____
_____
_____
_____
_____

What is your favorite season of the year?

Person 1:

_____
_____
_____
_____
_____
_____
_____

Person 2:

_____
_____
_____
_____
_____
_____
_____

Date:

....

What song would you choose for your funeral?

Person 1:

_____
_____
_____
_____
_____
_____
_____

Person 2:

_____
_____
_____
_____
_____
_____

What is your favorite alcohol?

Person 1:

_____

_____

_____

_____

_____

_____

_____

Person 2:

_____

_____

_____

_____

_____

_____

_____

Date:

....

What most tunes you to sex?

Person 1:

_____
_____
_____
_____
_____
_____
_____

Person 2:

_____
_____
_____
_____
_____
_____

Date:

....

What is your favorite day of the week?

Person 1:

_____
_____
_____
_____
_____
_____
_____

Person 2:

_____
_____
_____
_____
_____
_____

Are you a dog or cat person?

Person 1:

_____
_____
_____
_____
_____
_____
_____

Person 2:

_____
_____
_____
_____
_____

Date:

....

What is your favorite holiday?

Person 1:

_____
_____
_____
_____
_____
_____
_____

Person 2:

_____
_____
_____
_____
_____
_____
_____

Date:

....

What do you prefer: coffee or tea?

Person 1:

_____

_____

_____

_____

_____

_____

_____

Person 2:

_____

_____

_____

_____

_____

Date:

....

What do you like most during sex?

Person 1:

_____

_____

_____

_____

_____

_____

_____

Person 2:

_____

_____

_____

_____

_____

_____

Date:

....

What is your favorite literary genre?

Person 1:

_____

_____

_____

_____

_____

_____

_____

Person 2:

_____

_____

_____

_____

_____

_____

Date:

....

List three countries you would like to visit.

Person 1:

_____

_____

_____

_____

_____

_____

Person 2:

_____

_____

_____

_____

_____

_____

What is your favorite movie genre?

Person 1:

_____

_____

_____

_____

_____

_____

_____

Person 2:

_____

_____

_____

_____

_____

_____

Do you prefer sex in the morning or evening?

Person 1:

_____

_____

_____

_____

_____

_____

Person 2:

_____

_____

_____

_____

_____

Date:

....

Where would you like to have your grave?

Person 1:

_____

_____

_____

_____

_____

_____

_____

Person 2:

_____

_____

_____

_____

_____

_____

Date:

....

Do you believe in UFOs?

Person 1:

_____

_____

_____

_____

_____

_____

_____

Person 2:

_____

_____

_____

_____

_____

_____

_____

Date:

....

What is your favorite book?

Person 1:

_____
_____
_____
_____
_____
_____
_____

Person 2:

_____
_____
_____
_____
_____
_____

How would you like to spend the holiday of your dreams?

Person 1:

_____
_____
_____
_____
_____
_____
_____

Person 2:

_____
_____
_____
_____
_____
_____

What is your greatest passion?

Person 1:

_____

_____

_____

_____

_____

_____

_____

Person 2:

_____

_____

_____

_____

_____

_____

Date:

....

What are you ashamed of during sex?

Person 1:

_____
_____
_____
_____
_____
_____
_____

Person 2:

_____
_____
_____
_____
_____
_____

Date:

....

Would you rather be too thin or obese?

Person 1:

_____

_____

_____

_____

_____

_____

_____

Person 2:

_____

_____

_____

_____

_____

Date:

....

What is your favorite way to waste time?

Person 1:

_____

_____

_____

_____

_____

_____

_____

Person 2:

_____

_____

_____

_____

_____

_____

You have $ 50,000 to spend at once, what do you do with that amount?

Person 1:

_____
_____
_____
_____
_____
_____
_____

Person 2:

_____
_____
_____
_____
_____

Do you prefer to cook or wash?

Person 1:

_____
_____
_____
_____
_____
_____
_____
_____

Person 2:

_____
_____
_____
_____
_____
_____
_____

What do you like to do in your free time?

Person 1:

_____
_____
_____
_____
_____
_____
_____

Person 2:

_____
_____
_____
_____
_____
_____

If you had to change your profession, what would you do instead?

Person 1:

_____
_____
_____
_____
_____
_____
_____

Person 2:

_____
_____
_____
_____
_____
_____

What portion of your salary do you save?

Person 1:

_____

_____

_____

_____

_____

_____

_____

Person 2:

_____

_____

_____

_____

_____

_____

Date:

....

What are you afra-id of the most?

Person 1:

_____
_____
_____
_____
_____
_____
_____

Person 2:

_____
_____
_____
_____
_____
_____

What is your favorite actor?

Person 1:

_____

_____

_____

_____

_____

_____

_____

Person 2:

_____

_____

_____

_____

_____

Date:

....

Who do you look like the most?

Person 1:

_____

_____

_____

_____

_____

_____

_____

Person 2:

_____

_____

_____

_____

_____

_____

_____

What is your favorite actress?

Person 1:

_____

_____

_____

_____

_____

_____

_____

Person 2:

_____

_____

_____

_____

_____

_____

Are you afraid of death? Why?

Person 1:

_____
_____
_____
_____
_____
_____
_____
_____

Person 2:

_____
_____
_____
_____
_____
_____

Date:

....

What is your most precious souvenir?

Person 1:

_____
_____
_____
_____
_____
_____

Person 2:

_____
_____
_____
_____
_____

Date:

....

What do you love your partner for?

Person 1:

_____
_____
_____
_____
_____
_____
_____
_____

Person 2:

_____
_____
_____
_____
_____
_____
_____

Where do you like shopping the most?

Person 1:

_____
_____
_____
_____
_____
_____
_____

Person 2:

_____
_____
_____
_____
_____
_____

Are you afraid to become old?

Person 1:

_____

_____

_____

_____

_____

_____

_____

Person 2:

_____

_____

_____

_____

_____

_____

What do you think your partner likes to do the most?

Person 1:

_____
_____
_____
_____
_____
_____
_____

Person 2:

_____
_____
_____
_____
_____

What does sex mean to you?

Person 1:

_____
_____
_____
_____
_____
_____
_____

Person 2:

_____
_____
_____
_____
_____
_____

Date:

....

What do you think makes your partner laugh the most?

Person 1:

_____
_____
_____
_____
_____
_____
_____

Person 2:

_____
_____
_____
_____
_____

Date:

....

What you don't like about your job?

Person 1:

_____
_____
_____
_____
_____
_____
_____

Person 2:

_____
_____
_____
_____
_____
_____

Date:

....

What do you think annoys your partner the most?

Person 1:

_____
_____
_____
_____
_____
_____
_____

Person 2:

_____
_____
_____
_____
_____
_____

Date:

....

In sex, you prefer to dominate or be passive?

Person 1:

_____
_____
_____
_____
_____
_____
_____

Person 2:

_____
_____
_____
_____
_____
_____

What makes you feel better?

Person 1:

_____
_____
_____
_____
_____
_____
_____

Person 2:

_____
_____
_____
_____
_____
_____

Date:

....

What do you like in your life?

Person 1:

_____
_____
_____
_____
_____
_____
_____

Person 2:

_____
_____
_____
_____
_____
_____

Date:

....

What inspires you the most?

Person 1:

_____
_____
_____
_____
_____
_____
_____

Person 2:

_____
_____
_____
_____
_____

If you were to set up a company - what would it be?

Person 1:

_____

_____

_____

_____

_____

_____

_____

Person 2:

_____

_____

_____

_____

_____

_____

Date:

....

What habits would you like to implement in your life?

Person 1:

_____

_____

_____

_____

_____

_____

_____

Person 2:

_____

_____

_____

_____

_____

What do you think upsets your partner the most?

Person 1:

_____
_____
_____
_____
_____
_____
_____

Person 2:

_____
_____
_____
_____
_____
_____

Date:

....

What do you like about your job?

Person 1:

_____

_____

_____

_____

_____

_____

_____

Person 2:

_____

_____

_____

_____

_____

_____

What do you take strength from?

Person 1:

_____
_____
_____
_____
_____
_____
_____

Person 2:

_____
_____
_____
_____
_____
_____

What you don't like in your life?

Person 1:

_____

_____

_____

_____

_____

_____

_____

Person 2:

_____

_____

_____

_____

_____

How often do you masturbate?

Person 1:

_____
_____
_____
_____
_____
_____
_____

Person 2:

_____
_____
_____
_____
_____
_____

Date:

....

What is your favorite sport?

Person 1:

_____
_____
_____
_____
_____
_____
_____

Person 2:

_____
_____
_____
_____
_____
_____

What habits would you like to remove from your life?

Person 1:

_____

_____

_____

_____

_____

_____

_____

_____

Person 2:

_____

_____

_____

_____

_____

_____

_____

Date:

....

What motivates you the most?

Person 1:

_____

_____

_____

_____

_____

_____

_____

Person 2:

_____

_____

_____

_____

_____

_____

Are you happy?

Person 1:

_____
_____
_____
_____
_____
_____
_____

Person 2:

_____
_____
_____
_____
_____
_____

Date:

....

What do you lack most in life?

Person 1:

_____
_____
_____
_____
_____
_____
_____

Person 2:

_____
_____
_____
_____
_____
_____

Date:

....

What is your specialty dish?

Person 1:

_____
_____
_____
_____
_____
_____
_____

Person 2:

_____
_____
_____
_____
_____
_____

Date:

....

What habits should your partner get rid of?

Person 1:

_____

_____

_____

_____

_____

_____

_____

Person 2:

_____

_____

_____

_____

_____

_____

Date:

....

What habits should your partner learn?

Person 1:

_____
_____
_____
_____
_____
_____
_____
_____

Person 2:

_____
_____
_____
_____
_____
_____
_____

Date:

....

How do you take care of your health?

Person 1:

_____

_____

_____

_____

_____

_____

_____

Person 2:

_____

_____

_____

_____

_____

_____

Date:

....

What sound do you like the most?

Person 1:

_____

_____

_____

_____

_____

_____

_____

Person 2:

_____

_____

_____

_____

_____

_____

What do you associate with holidays?

Person 1:

_____

_____

_____

_____

_____

_____

_____

Person 2:

_____

_____

_____

_____

_____

_____

What stresses you the most?

Person 1:

_____

_____

_____

_____

_____

_____

_____

Person 2:

_____

_____

_____

_____

_____

_____

What dish do you associate with childhood?

Person 1:

_____

_____

_____

_____

_____

_____

_____

Person 2:

_____

_____

_____

_____

_____

_____

What stresses your partner the most?

Person 1:

_____
_____
_____
_____
_____
_____
_____

Person 2:

_____
_____
_____
_____
_____
_____

What do you usually eat? What is your diet?

Person 1:

_____
_____
_____
_____
_____
_____
_____

Person 2:

_____
_____
_____
_____
_____

What may your partner miss most in life?

Person 1:

_____

_____

_____

_____

_____

_____

_____

Person 2:

_____

_____

_____

_____

_____

_____

Date:

....

What do you usually cook for your partner?

Person 1:

_____

_____

_____

_____

_____

_____

Person 2:

_____

_____

_____

_____

_____

Date:

....

What is your favorite fragrance?

Person 1:

_____

_____

_____

_____

_____

_____

_____

Person 2:

_____

_____

_____

_____

_____

_____

Date:

....

What relaxes you the most?

Person 1:

_____
_____
_____
_____
_____
_____
_____

Person 2:

_____
_____
_____
_____
_____
_____

Date:

....

What did you like to do as a child?

Person 1:

_____
_____
_____
_____
_____
_____
_____

Person 2:

_____
_____
_____
_____
_____
_____

Who is your authority?

Person 1:

_____

_____

_____

_____

_____

_____

_____

Person 2:

_____

_____

_____

_____

_____

_____

Date:

....

What is your dream car?

Person 1:

_____

_____

_____

_____

_____

_____

_____

Person 2:

_____

_____

_____

_____

_____

_____

_____

Date:

....

What is your most beautiful childhood memory?

Person 1:

_____

_____

_____

_____

_____

_____

_____

Person 2:

_____

_____

_____

_____

_____

_____

What does your partner wear most often?

Person 1:

_____

_____

_____

_____

_____

_____

_____

Person 2:

_____

_____

_____

_____

_____

_____

_____

What did you want to achieve when you were little?

Person 1:

_____
_____
_____
_____
_____
_____
_____
_____

Person 2:

_____
_____
_____
_____
_____

Which holiday you remember as the best one?

Person 1:

_____

_____

_____

_____

_____

_____

_____

Person 2:

_____

_____

_____

_____

_____

_____

_____

What relaxes your partner the most?

Person 1:

_____

_____

_____

_____

_____

_____

_____

Person 2:

_____

_____

_____

_____

_____

_____

Who influenced you the most in your childhood?

Person 1:

_____
_____
_____
_____
_____
_____
_____
_____

Person 2:

_____
_____
_____
_____
_____
_____
_____

Date:

....

What is your favorite outfit?

Person 1:

_____
_____
_____
_____
_____
_____
_____

Person 2:

_____
_____
_____
_____
_____
_____

Date:

....

What is your dream home?

Person 1:

_____
_____
_____
_____
_____
_____
_____
_____

Person 2:

_____
_____
_____
_____
_____
_____
_____

Date:

....

You are more of
an introvert or extrovert?

Person 1:

_____

_____

_____

_____

_____

_____

_____

Person 2:

_____

_____

_____

_____

_____

_____

Who influenced you the most in your youth?

Person 1:

_____
_____
_____
_____
_____
_____
_____

Person 2:

_____
_____
_____
_____
_____
_____

What body part do you like to have the most massaged?

Person 1:

_____
_____
_____
_____
_____
_____
_____

Person 2:

_____
_____
_____
_____
_____
_____

How do you like to comb your hair the most?

Person 1:

_____

_____

_____

_____

_____

_____

_____

Person 2:

_____

_____

_____

_____

_____

_____

Date:

....

Imagine you can visit only one continent. Which one would you choose?

Person 1:

_____
_____
_____
_____
_____
_____
_____

Person 2:

_____
_____
_____
_____
_____
_____

Date:

....

Do you believe in ghosts?

Person 1:

_____
_____
_____
_____
_____
_____
_____
_____

Person 2:

_____
_____
_____
_____
_____
_____
_____

Date:

....

What is your favorite car model?

Person 1:

_____

_____

_____

_____

_____

_____

_____

Person 2:

_____

_____

_____

_____

_____

_____

Date:

....

What does your partner must always have with him/her?

Person 1:

_____
_____
_____
_____
_____
_____
_____

Person 2:

_____
_____
_____
_____
_____
_____

Date:

....

What is your partner most afraid of?

Person 1:

_____
_____
_____
_____
_____
_____
_____

Person 2:

_____
_____
_____
_____
_____
_____

How long was the longest period during which you did not see each other?

Person 1:

_____

_____

_____

_____

_____

_____

_____

Person 2:

_____

_____

_____

_____

_____

_____

What tree do you associate with your partner?

Person 1:

_____
_____
_____
_____
_____
_____
_____

Person 2:

_____
_____
_____
_____
_____
_____

Date:

....

What are your favorite flowers?

Person 1:

_____

_____

_____

_____

_____

_____

_____

Person 2:

_____

_____

_____

_____

_____

_____

What does loyalty mean to you?

Person 1:

_____

_____

_____

_____

_____

_____

_____

Person 2:

_____

_____

_____

_____

_____

_____

Do you believe in love for life?

Person 1:

_____

_____

_____

_____

_____

_____

_____

Person 2:

_____

_____

_____

_____

_____

_____

_____

How soon do you start missing your partner?

Person 1:

_____
_____
_____
_____
_____
_____
_____

Person 2:

_____
_____
_____
_____
_____

What bird do you associate with your partner?

Person 1:

_____
_____
_____
_____
_____
_____
_____

Person 2:

_____
_____
_____
_____
_____
_____

Date:

....

Do you believe in love at first sight?

Person 1:

_____
_____
_____
_____
_____
_____
_____

Person 2:

_____
_____
_____
_____
_____
_____

Date:

....

What does friendship mean to you?

Person 1:

_____

_____

_____

_____

_____

_____

_____

Person 2:

_____

_____

_____

_____

_____

_____

Date:

....

What makes you miss your partner?

Person 1:

_____
_____
_____
_____
_____
_____
_____

Person 2:

_____
_____
_____
_____
_____
_____

Date:

....

What are your favorite sweets?

Person 1:

_____

_____

_____

_____

_____

_____

_____

Person 2:

_____

_____

_____

_____

_____

_____

Date:

....

What is your favorite place to walk?

Person 1:

_____
_____
_____
_____
_____
_____
_____

Person 2:

_____
_____
_____
_____
_____

Date:

....

What are your plans for tonight?

Person 1:

_____
_____
_____
_____
_____
_____
_____
_____

Person 2:

_____
_____
_____
_____
_____
_____

What do you like most about your sex?

Person 1:

_____

_____

_____

_____

_____

_____

Person 2:

_____

_____

_____

_____

_____

_____

For what do you like yourself the most?

Person 1:

_____

_____

_____

_____

_____

_____

_____

Person 2:

_____

_____

_____

_____

_____

_____

Date:

....

Where would you like to take your partner?

Person 1:

_____

_____

_____

_____

_____

_____

_____

Person 2:

_____

_____

_____

_____

_____

_____

Date:

....

What does your partner usually do after work?

Person 1:

_____
_____
_____
_____
_____
_____
_____

Person 2:

_____
_____
_____
_____
_____
_____

What would you like to change in yourself?

Person 1:

_____

_____

_____

_____

_____

_____

_____

Person 2:

_____

_____

_____

_____

_____

_____

Date:

....

Do you prefer traditional books or ebooks?

Person 1:

_____

_____

_____

_____

_____

_____

_____

Person 2:

_____

_____

_____

_____

_____

What was your the worst nightmare?

Person 1:

_____
_____
_____
_____
_____
_____
_____

Person 2:

_____
_____
_____
_____
_____
_____

Date:

....

What were you afraid of as a child?

Person 1:

_____

_____

_____

_____

_____

_____

_____

Person 2:

_____

_____

_____

_____

_____

_____

Which room in your home do you like the most?

Person 1:

_____
_____
_____
_____
_____
_____

Person 2:

_____
_____
_____
_____
_____

Have you ever watched porn?

Person 1:

_____
_____
_____
_____
_____
_____
_____
_____

Person 2:

_____
_____
_____
_____
_____
_____

What was the strangest thing that your partner did during sleep?

Person 1:

_____

_____

_____

_____

_____

_____

_____

Person 2:

_____

_____

_____

_____

_____

_____

What is your favorite TV program?

Person 1:

_____

_____

_____

_____

_____

_____

_____

Person 2:

_____

_____

_____

_____

_____

_____

Have you ever been to a sex shop?

Person 1:

_____
_____
_____
_____
_____
_____
_____

Person 2:

_____
_____
_____
_____
_____
_____
_____

In which room of your home your partner stays most often?

Person 1:

_____
_____
_____
_____
_____
_____
_____

Person 2:

_____
_____
_____
_____
_____
_____

Date:

....

What do you talk about most often?

Person 1:

_____
_____
_____
_____
_____
_____
_____

Person 2:

_____
_____
_____
_____
_____
_____

What have you not tried in bed yet, and would like to?

Person 1:

_____
_____
_____
_____
_____
_____
_____

Person 2:

_____
_____
_____
_____
_____
_____

What is your shared passion?

Person 1:

_____

_____

_____

_____

_____

_____

_____

Person 2:

_____

_____

_____

_____

_____

What do you like to do most with your partner?

Person 1:

_____

_____

_____

_____

_____

_____

_____

Person 2:

_____

_____

_____

_____

_____

_____

What do you usually dream about?

Person 1:

_____

_____

_____

_____

_____

_____

_____

Person 2:

_____

_____

_____

_____

_____

_____

Date:

....

Do you prefer to sleep on a hard or soft mattress?

Person 1:

_____

_____

_____

_____

_____

_____

_____

Person 2:

_____

_____

_____

_____

_____

_____

Have you ever pissed yourself laughing? What was the situation?

Person 1:

_____

_____

_____

_____

_____

_____

_____

Person 2:

_____

_____

_____

_____

_____

Date:

....

How do you like to spend time with your partner the most?

Person 1:

_____

_____

_____

_____

_____

_____

_____

Person 2:

_____

_____

_____

_____

_____

_____

What was your most beautiful dream?

Person 1:

_____

_____

_____

_____

_____

_____

_____

Person 2:

_____

_____

_____

_____

_____

Do you like erotic toys?

Person 1:

_____

_____

_____

_____

_____

_____

_____

Person 2:

_____

_____

_____

_____

_____

_____

Date:

....

What is your role model for you?

Person 1:

_____
_____
_____
_____
_____
_____
_____

Person 2:

_____
_____
_____
_____
_____
_____

What is your dream hotel to spend the night?

Person 1:

_____
_____
_____
_____
_____
_____
_____

Person 2:

_____
_____
_____
_____
_____
_____

Date:

....

What upsets your partner the most?

Person 1:

_____

_____

_____

_____

_____

_____

_____

Person 2:

_____

_____

_____

_____

_____

_____

What was the craziest thing you've ever done?

Person 1:

_____
_____
_____
_____
_____
_____
_____

Person 2:

_____
_____
_____
_____
_____
_____

What upsets you the most?

Person 1:

_____
_____
_____
_____
_____
_____
_____

Person 2:

_____
_____
_____
_____
_____

Date:

....

What was the most romantic thing you did for your partner?

Person 1:

_____
_____
_____
_____
_____
_____
_____

Person 2:

_____
_____
_____
_____
_____
_____

Date:

....

How often do you talk to each other?

Person 1:

_____

_____

_____

_____

_____

_____

_____

Person 2:

_____

_____

_____

_____

_____

_____

_____

Date:

....

Who was the most important person for you in your youth?

Person 1:

_____

_____

_____

_____

_____

_____

_____

Person 2:

_____

_____

_____

_____

_____

_____

How much time a week do you spend together and without anyone else?

Person 1:

_____

_____

_____

_____

_____

_____

_____

Person 2:

_____

_____

_____

_____

_____

Date:

....

What would you like to improve in your relationship?

Person 1:

_____

_____

_____

_____

_____

_____

_____

Person 2:

_____

_____

_____

_____

_____

_____

Date:

....

For what are you thankful the most to your mother?

Person 1:

_____

_____

_____

_____

_____

_____

_____

_____

Person 2:

_____

_____

_____

_____

_____

_____

Date:

....

For what are you thankful the most to your father?

Person 1:

_____
_____
_____
_____
_____
_____
_____
_____

Person 2:

_____
_____
_____
_____
_____
_____

Date:

....

What are you most proud of?

Person 1:

_____
_____
_____
_____
_____
_____
_____

Person 2:

_____
_____
_____
_____
_____
_____

If you met the president, what would you tell him?

Person 1:

_____

_____

_____

_____

_____

_____

_____

Person 2:

_____

_____

_____

_____

_____

Date:

....

What kind of parent would you like to be for your children?

Person 1:

_____

_____

_____

_____

_____

_____

_____

Person 2:

_____

_____

_____

_____

_____

_____

Date:

....

How would you like people to remember you?

Person 1:

_____

_____

_____

_____

_____

_____

_____

Person 2:

_____

_____

_____

_____

_____

What do you like about your parents' relationship?

Person 1:

_____

_____

_____

_____

_____

_____

_____

Person 2:

_____

_____

_____

_____

_____

Date:

....

What is the most important thing to do today?

Person 1:

_____
_____
_____
_____
_____
_____
_____

Person 2:

_____
_____
_____
_____
_____
_____

What you don't like about your parents' relationship?

Person 1:

_____
_____
_____
_____
_____
_____
_____

Person 2:

_____
_____
_____
_____
_____
_____

Date:

....

What you don't like doing?

Person 1:

_____
_____
_____
_____
_____
_____
_____

Person 2:

_____
_____
_____
_____
_____
_____

Who is your best friend?

Person 1:

_____
_____
_____
_____
_____
_____
_____

Person 2:

_____
_____
_____
_____
_____
_____

Date:

....

What is your fulfilled childhood dream that you would like to do once again?

Person 1:

_____

_____

_____

_____

_____

_____

_____

Person 2:

_____

_____

_____

_____

_____

Date:

....

Who you don't like talking to?

Person 1:

_____
_____
_____
_____
_____
_____
_____

Person 2:

_____
_____
_____
_____
_____
_____

Date:

....

Do you believe in magic?

Person 1:

_____

_____

_____

_____

_____

_____

_____

_____

Person 2:

_____

_____

_____

_____

_____

_____

_____

_____

Which politician do you like the most?

Person 1:

_____

_____

_____

_____

_____

_____

Person 2:

_____

_____

_____

_____

_____

How should your country look like in 20 years?

Person 1:

_____

_____

_____

_____

_____

_____

_____

Person 2:

_____

_____

_____

_____

_____

_____

Date:

....

How was your day?

Person 1:

_____

_____

_____

_____

_____

_____

_____

Person 2:

_____

_____

_____

_____

_____

_____

What do you do on a daily basis to be more eco?

Person 1:

_____

_____

_____

_____

_____

_____

_____

Person 2:

_____

_____

_____

_____

_____

Date:

....

How would you like your funeral to look like?

Person 1:

_____
_____
_____
_____
_____
_____
_____

Person 2:

_____
_____
_____
_____
_____

Date:

....

Describe your
perfect morning.

Person 1:

_____
_____
_____
_____
_____
_____
_____
_____

Person 2:

_____
_____
_____
_____
_____
_____

Describe your perfect evening.

Person 1:

_____
_____
_____
_____
_____
_____
_____

Person 2:

_____
_____
_____
_____
_____
_____

Have you ever spent the night under the stars?

Person 1:

_____
_____
_____
_____
_____
_____
_____

Person 2:

_____
_____
_____
_____
_____
_____

Date:

....

Describe your perfect afternoon.

Person 1:

_____
_____
_____
_____
_____
_____
_____

Person 2:

_____
_____
_____
_____
_____

Date:

....

What is your goal for this year?

Person 1:

_____

_____

_____

_____

_____

_____

_____

Person 2:

_____

_____

_____

_____

_____

Date:

....

What would you like to do today?

Person 1:

_____
_____
_____
_____
_____
_____
_____

Person 2:

_____
_____
_____
_____
_____

Date:

....

Describe your perfect Sunday?

Person 1:

_____
_____
_____
_____
_____
_____
_____

Person 2:

_____
_____
_____
_____
_____
_____

Date:

....

What did you do for your health today?

Person 1:

_____

_____

_____

_____

_____

_____

Person 2:

_____

_____

_____

_____

_____

Where would you never want to go?

Person 1:

_____
_____
_____
_____
_____
_____
_____

Person 2:

_____
_____
_____
_____
_____
_____

Date:

....

What would you like to do with your partner today?

Person 1:

_____
_____
_____
_____
_____
_____
_____
_____

Person 2:

_____
_____
_____
_____
_____
_____

Date:

....

What animal are you most afraid of?

Person 1:

_____

_____

_____

_____

_____

_____

_____

Person 2:

_____

_____

_____

_____

_____

_____

Date:

....

What dish do you associate with your partner?

Person 1:

_____
_____
_____
_____
_____
_____
_____

Person 2:

_____
_____
_____
_____
_____
_____

Date:

....

What do you enjoy the most?

Person 1:

_____

_____

_____

_____

_____

_____

_____

Person 2:

_____

_____

_____

_____

_____

_____

What are you really good at?

Person 1:

_____
_____
_____
_____
_____
_____
_____

Person 2:

_____
_____
_____
_____
_____
_____

Date:

....

What place would you never want to visit?

Person 1:

_____

_____

_____

_____

_____

_____

_____

Person 2:

_____

_____

_____

_____

_____

_____

Date:

....

If you could have magical abilities, what would it be?

Person 1:

_____
_____
_____
_____
_____
_____
_____

Person 2:

_____
_____
_____
_____
_____
_____

Date:

....

If you could change one thing in the world, what would it be?

Person 1:

_____

_____

_____

_____

_____

_____

_____

_____

Person 2:

_____

_____

_____

_____

_____

_____

If you became president, what would be the first thing you would do?

Person 1:

_____
_____
_____
_____
_____
_____
_____

Person 2:

_____
_____
_____
_____
_____
_____

Have you ever wanted to be famous?

Person 1:

_____

_____

_____

_____

_____

_____

_____

Person 2:

_____

_____

_____

_____

_____

What is the most exciting for you?

Person 1:

_____

_____

_____

_____

_____

_____

_____

Person 2:

_____

_____

_____

_____

_____

_____

Date:

....

When was the last time you told your partner that you loved him?

Person 1:

_____
_____
_____
_____
_____
_____
_____

Person 2:

_____
_____
_____
_____
_____

Date:

....

What compliment do you usually tell your partner?

Person 1:

_____
_____
_____
_____
_____
_____
_____

Person 2:

_____
_____
_____
_____
_____

Date:

....

Who usually cleans your home?

Person 1:

_____

_____

_____

_____

_____

_____

_____

Person 2:

_____

_____

_____

_____

_____

_____

What superpower do you think your partner would like to have?

Person 1:

_____
_____
_____
_____
_____
_____
_____

Person 2:

_____
_____
_____
_____
_____

Date:

....

What was the coolest surprise you made for your partner?

Person 1:

_____

_____

_____

_____

_____

_____

_____

Person 2:

_____

_____

_____

_____

_____

Date:

....

What would you like to get from your partner for the next occasion?

Person 1:

_____

_____

_____

_____

_____

_____

_____

Person 2:

_____

_____

_____

_____

_____

_____

Date:

....

Last time you said something nice to your partner...?

Person 1:

_____
_____
_____
_____
_____
_____
_____

Person 2:

_____
_____
_____
_____
_____
_____

Date:

....

When do you celebrate your anniversary?

Person 1:

_____

_____

_____

_____

_____

_____

_____

_____

Person 2:

_____

_____

_____

_____

_____

_____

What compliment you usually hear from your partner?

Person 1:

_____
_____
_____
_____
_____
_____
_____

Person 2:

_____
_____
_____
_____
_____
_____

Is there anything you would like your partner not to tell you?

Person 1:

_____

_____

_____

_____

_____

_____

_____

Person 2:

_____

_____

_____

_____

_____

_____

Date:

....

When did you meet first time?

Person 1:

_____

_____

_____

_____

_____

_____

_____

Person 2:

_____

_____

_____

_____

_____

_____

Date:

....

How long have you been together?

Person 1:

_____
_____
_____
_____
_____
_____
_____

Person 2:

_____
_____
_____
_____
_____
_____

Date:

....

What is your
favorite restaurant?

Person 1:

_____

_____

_____

_____

_____

_____

_____

Person 2:

_____

_____

_____

_____

_____

_____

Date:

....

At what time were you born?

Person 1:

_____
_____
_____
_____
_____
_____
_____

Person 2:

_____
_____
_____
_____
_____
_____

Date:

....

What is your zodiac sign?

Person 1:

_____
_____
_____
_____
_____
_____
_____

Person 2:

_____
_____
_____
_____
_____
_____

What was the coolest surprise your partner made for you?

Person 1:

_____
_____
_____
_____
_____
_____
_____

Person 2:

_____
_____
_____
_____
_____

What is your spiritual animal?

Person 1:

_____
_____
_____
_____
_____
_____
_____

Person 2:

_____
_____
_____
_____
_____
_____

When was the last time you cooked something for your partner?

Person 1:

_____

_____

_____

_____

_____

_____

_____

Person 2:

_____

_____

_____

_____

_____

_____

Date:

....

What would you like to hear more often from your partner?

Person 1:

_____
_____
_____
_____
_____
_____
_____

Person 2:

_____
_____
_____
_____
_____
_____

Date:

....

What was your first word?

Person 1:

_____
_____
_____
_____
_____
_____
_____
_____

Person 2:

_____
_____
_____
_____
_____
_____

What kind of gift have you recently bought your partner?

Person 1:

_____
_____
_____
_____
_____
_____
_____

Person 2:

_____
_____
_____
_____
_____
_____

What is your dream president?

Person 1:

_____
_____
_____
_____
_____
_____
_____

Person 2:

_____
_____
_____
_____
_____

Date:

....

Have you ever wanted to be an actor / singer?

Person 1:

_____

_____

_____

_____

_____

_____

_____

Person 2:

_____

_____

_____

_____

_____

How do you approach public speaking?

Person 1:

_____
_____
_____
_____
_____
_____
_____

Person 2:

_____
_____
_____
_____
_____
_____

What creative things can you do?

Person 1:

_____
_____
_____
_____
_____
_____
_____

Person 2:

_____
_____
_____
_____
_____

Date:

....

How often do you clean your home?

Person 1:

_____
_____
_____
_____
_____
_____
_____

Person 2:

_____
_____
_____
_____
_____

Have you ever wanted to be a politician?

Person 1:

_____
_____
_____
_____
_____
_____
_____

Person 2:

_____
_____
_____
_____
_____
_____

Who cooks more often?

Person 1:

_____

_____

_____

_____

_____

_____

_____

Person 2:

_____

_____

_____

_____

_____

_____

Who in your relationship is a greater mess?

Person 1:

_____

_____

_____

_____

_____

_____

_____

Person 2:

_____

_____

_____

_____

_____

What is your Chinese zodiac sign?

Person 1:

_____

_____

_____

_____

_____

_____

_____

Person 2:

_____

_____

_____

_____

_____

_____

_____

Where your partner likes to be massaged?

Person 1:

_____
_____
_____
_____
_____
_____
_____

Person 2:

_____
_____
_____
_____
_____
_____

Date:

....

What usually annoys you?

Person 1:

_____
_____
_____
_____
_____
_____
_____

Person 2:

_____
_____
_____
_____
_____

Date:

....

What style of houses / flats do you like?

Person 1:

_____
_____
_____
_____
_____
_____
_____

Person 2:

_____
_____
_____
_____
_____
_____

What do your parents like your partner for?

Person 1:

_____

_____

_____

_____

_____

_____

_____

Person 2:

_____

_____

_____

_____

_____

_____

What was the craziest thing you did together?

Person 1:

_____
_____
_____
_____
_____
_____
_____
_____

Person 2:

_____
_____
_____
_____
_____
_____
_____

Date:

....

How zero waste is your home?

Person 1:

_____
_____
_____
_____
_____
_____
_____
_____

Person 2:

_____
_____
_____
_____
_____
_____
_____

What are your partner's strongest erogenous zones?

Person 1:

_____
_____
_____
_____
_____
_____
_____
_____

Person 2:

_____
_____
_____
_____
_____
_____
_____

What was the most stupid thing you did together?

Person 1:

_____

_____

_____

_____

_____

_____

_____

Person 2:

_____

_____

_____

_____

_____

Date:

....

When do you like to be alone?

Person 1:

_____
_____
_____
_____
_____
_____
_____
_____

Person 2:

_____
_____
_____
_____
_____
_____
_____
_____

At what times do you most need your partner's presence?

Person 1:

_____

_____

_____

_____

_____

_____

_____

Person 2:

_____

_____

_____

_____

_____

_____

Date:

....

Sweet or salty food?

Person 1:

_____

_____

_____

_____

_____

_____

_____

Person 2:

_____

_____

_____

_____

Date:

....

Who spends the most money on shopping?

Person 1:

_____
_____
_____
_____
_____
_____
_____

Person 2:

_____
_____
_____
_____
_____
_____

What was the strangest thing that your partner did?

Person 1:

_____
_____
_____
_____
_____
_____
_____

Person 2:

_____
_____
_____
_____
_____

In what moments your partner likes to be alone?

Person 1:

_____
_____
_____
_____
_____
_____
_____

Person 2:

_____
_____
_____
_____
_____

What is your favorite flavor of ice cream?

Person 1:

_____
_____
_____
_____
_____
_____
_____

Person 2:

_____
_____
_____
_____
_____

Which one of you is late more often?

Person 1:

_____
_____
_____
_____
_____
_____
_____

Person 2:

_____
_____
_____
_____
_____
_____

Date:

....

How old were you when you obtained your driver's license?

Person 1:

_____
_____
_____
_____
_____
_____
_____

Person 2:

_____
_____
_____
_____
_____

At what times does your partner need your presence?

Person 1:

_____
_____
_____
_____
_____
_____
_____

Person 2:

_____
_____
_____
_____
_____
_____

What is your partner's favorite dessert?

Person 1:

_____
_____
_____
_____
_____
_____
_____

Person 2:

_____
_____
_____
_____
_____

Which one of you has the habit of talking to yourself?

Person 1:

_____
_____
_____
_____
_____
_____
_____

Person 2:

_____
_____
_____
_____
_____

Date:

....

Who makes groceries most often?

Person 1:

_____

_____

_____

_____

_____

_____

_____

Person 2:

_____

_____

_____

_____

_____

_____

What was your most distant journey?

Person 1:

_____

_____

_____

_____

_____

_____

_____

Person 2:

_____

_____

_____

_____

_____

Date:

....

Which one of you knows your family history better?

Person 1:

_____

_____

_____

_____

_____

_____

_____

Person 2:

_____

_____

_____

_____

_____

Date:

....

Do you have your unique place?

Person 1:

_____
_____
_____
_____
_____
_____
_____

Person 2:

_____
_____
_____
_____
_____
_____

Date:

....

How do you imagine your perfect wedding anniversary?

Person 1:

_____

_____

_____

_____

_____

_____

_____

Person 2:

_____

_____

_____

_____

_____

Date:

....

What does your partner like to eat for breakfast?

Person 1:

_____
_____
_____
_____
_____
_____
_____

Person 2:

_____
_____
_____
_____
_____

How much do you think your partner should earn?

Person 1:

_____

_____

_____

_____

_____

_____

_____

Person 2:

_____

_____

_____

_____

_____

_____

Who in your family annoys your partner most often?

Person 1:

_____
_____
_____
_____
_____
_____
_____

Person 2:

_____
_____
_____
_____
_____

Date:

....

Who works more harder in your relationship?

Person 1:

_____
_____
_____
_____
_____
_____
_____

Person 2:

_____
_____
_____
_____
_____

Date:

....

What was the longest route that you traveled by car?

Person 1:

_____
_____
_____
_____
_____
_____
_____

Person 2:

_____
_____
_____
_____
_____
_____

Date:

....

What do you do every day to help your partner?

Person 1:

_____
_____
_____
_____
_____
_____
_____

Person 2:

_____
_____
_____
_____
_____

Date:

....

What do you like to eat for dinner?

Person 1:

_____

_____

_____

_____

_____

_____

_____

Person 2:

_____

_____

_____

_____

_____

Who in your family has not yet met your partner?

Person 1:

_____
_____
_____
_____
_____
_____
_____

Person 2:

_____
_____
_____
_____
_____
_____

Is there anything you are ashamed of that you wouldn't like to tell your partner about?

Person 1:

_____

_____

_____

_____

_____

_____

Person 2:

_____

_____

_____

_____

_____

What is your dream dinner?

Person 1:

_____

_____

_____

_____

_____

_____

_____

Person 2:

_____

_____

_____

_____

_____

Who annoys you most often in your family?

Person 1:

_____

_____

_____

_____

_____

_____

_____

Person 2:

_____

_____

_____

_____

_____

_____

Which one of you is a better driver?

Person 1:

_____
_____
_____
_____
_____
_____
_____

Person 2:

_____
_____
_____
_____
_____
_____
_____

Date:

....

What is your temperament?

Person 1:

_____

_____

_____

_____

_____

_____

_____

Person 2:

_____

_____

_____

_____

_____

What do you like to help your partner with?

Person 1:

_____
_____
_____
_____
_____
_____
_____

Person 2:

_____
_____
_____
_____
_____
_____

What do you find most difficult in everyday life?

Person 1:

_____
_____
_____
_____
_____
_____
_____

Person 2:

_____
_____
_____
_____
_____
_____

Describe the nature of your partner in 5 words.

Person 1:

_____
_____
_____
_____
_____
_____
_____

Person 2:

_____
_____
_____
_____
_____
_____

Date:

....

Who among you has a greater sense of humor?

Person 1:

_____

_____

_____

_____

_____

_____

_____

Person 2:

_____

_____

_____

_____

_____

What you don't like helping your partner with?

Person 1:

_____

_____

_____

_____

_____

_____

_____

Person 2:

_____

_____

_____

_____

_____

Date:

....

What kind of jokes amuse you the most?

Person 1:

_____

_____

_____

_____

_____

_____

Person 2:

_____

_____

_____

_____

_____

_____

How did you spend your honeymoon?

Person 1:

_____

_____

_____

_____

_____

_____

_____

_____

Person 2:

_____

_____

_____

_____

_____

_____

_____

Date:

....

Describe briefly how was your wedding / how do you imagine your wedding.

Person 1:

_____
_____
_____
_____
_____
_____
_____

Person 2:

_____
_____
_____
_____
_____
_____

What is the most difficult thing for your partner in everyday life?

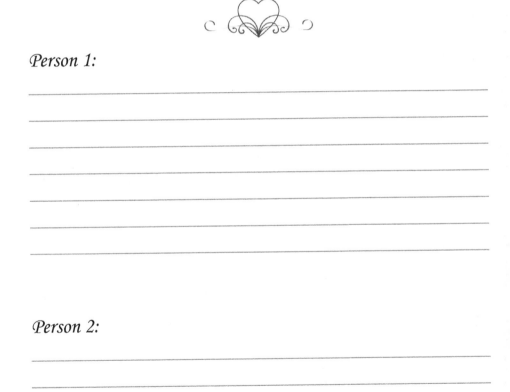

Person 1:

_____
_____
_____
_____
_____
_____
_____

Person 2:

_____
_____
_____
_____
_____
_____

Do you think that you are supporting your partner enough?

Person 1:

_____

_____

_____

_____

_____

_____

_____

Person 2:

_____

_____

_____

_____

_____

_____

Which one of you gets nervous faster?

Person 1:

_____
_____
_____
_____
_____
_____
_____

Person 2:

_____
_____
_____
_____
_____
_____

In your opinion, what kind of temperament does your partner have?

Person 1:

_____

_____

_____

_____

_____

_____

_____

Person 2:

_____

_____

_____

_____

_____

_____

Date:

....

Describe your character in 5 words.

Person 1:

_____
_____
_____
_____
_____
_____
_____

Person 2:

_____
_____
_____
_____
_____
_____

Who has a greater sense of humor?

Person 1:

_____

_____

_____

_____

_____

_____

_____

Person 2:

_____

_____

_____

_____

_____

_____

Date:

....

What would you say on your deathbed to your children?

Person 1:

_____

_____

_____

_____

_____

_____

_____

_____

Person 2:

_____

_____

_____

_____

_____

_____

Date:

....

Sightseeing or sunbathing?

Person 1:

_____

_____

_____

_____

_____

_____

_____

Person 2:

_____

_____

_____

_____

_____

_____

Who among you is more tanned?

Person 1:

_____

_____

_____

_____

_____

_____

_____

Person 2:

_____

_____

_____

_____

_____

_____

What type of jokes does your partner play most often?

Person 1:

_____

_____

_____

_____

_____

_____

_____

Person 2:

_____

_____

_____

_____

_____

_____

What would you say on your deathbed to your partner?

Person 1:

_____

_____

_____

_____

_____

_____

_____

Person 2:

_____

_____

_____

_____

_____

_____

Date:

....

Describe how was your engagement / how you would like your engagement to be.

Person 1:

_____

_____

_____

_____

_____

_____

_____

Person 2:

_____

_____

_____

_____

_____

_____

Date:

....

What would you like to hear from your partner just before your death?

Person 1:

_____
_____
_____
_____
_____
_____
_____
_____

Person 2:

_____
_____
_____
_____
_____

What animal would you never accept to have at home?

Person 1:

_____

_____

_____

_____

_____

_____

_____

Person 2:

_____

_____

_____

_____

_____

Date:

....

What was the stupidest thing you did in your childhood?

Person 1:

_____
_____
_____
_____
_____
_____
_____
_____

Person 2:

_____
_____
_____
_____
_____
_____

Date:

....

What was the situation where you were stressed the most?

Person 1:

_____

_____

_____

_____

_____

_____

_____

Person 2:

_____

_____

_____

_____

_____

_____

Camping or a luxury hotel?

Person 1:

_____

_____

_____

_____

_____

_____

_____

Person 2:

_____

_____

_____

_____

_____

_____

Date:

....

Who among you is more stable?

Person 1:

_____

_____

_____

_____

_____

_____

_____

Person 2:

_____

_____

_____

_____

_____

_____

Date:

....

What trait do you envy your partner?

Person 1:

_____

_____

_____

_____

_____

_____

_____

Person 2:

_____

_____

_____

_____

_____

_____

Which one of your partner's traits you would never accept?

Person 1:

_____
_____
_____
_____
_____
_____
_____

Person 2:

_____
_____
_____
_____
_____
_____

If you were to choose a different nationality for yourself, which one would it be?

Person 1:

_____

_____

_____

_____

_____

_____

_____

Person 2:

_____

_____

_____

_____

_____

_____

What do you like to eat for breakfast the most?

Person 1:

_____
_____
_____
_____
_____
_____
_____

Person 2:

_____
_____
_____
_____
_____
_____

Date:

....

Mountains or the sea?

Person 1:

_____

_____

_____

_____

_____

_____

_____

Person 2:

_____

_____

_____

_____

_____

Date:

....

How do you start the day?

Person 1:

_____
_____
_____
_____
_____
_____
_____

Person 2:

_____
_____
_____
_____
_____
_____

Date:

....

What should your partner always remember?

Person 1:

_____
_____
_____
_____
_____
_____
_____

Person 2:

_____
_____
_____
_____
_____

What animal would you like to have at home?

Person 1:

_____

_____

_____

_____

_____

_____

_____

Person 2:

_____

_____

_____

_____

_____

_____

Date:

....

What was the stupidest thing you did at work?

Person 1:

_____
_____
_____
_____
_____
_____
_____
_____

Person 2:

_____
_____
_____
_____
_____
_____

How do you imagine your perfect morning?

Person 1:

_____
_____
_____
_____
_____
_____
_____

Person 2:

_____
_____
_____
_____
_____
_____

How does your partner start the day?

Person 1:

_____
_____
_____
_____
_____
_____
_____

Person 2:

_____
_____
_____
_____
_____
_____

Date:

....

What will you do together tomorrow?

Person 1:

_____

_____

_____

_____

_____

_____

Person 2:

_____

_____

_____

_____

_____

_____

What do you feel
after this 365 days
experience?

Person 1

Write your summary here:

Person 2

Write your summary here:

_____

_____

_____

_____

_____

_____

_____

_____

_____

_____

_____

_____

_____

_____

_____

_____

_____

_____

Thank you for spending your time together.

If you are looking for more Q&A books, we invite you to see our products on Amazon.com.

Wish you all the best!

Lovofun Team

Made in the USA
Middletown, DE
10 May 2022

65607635R00209